The Amazing, Stupendous, Extraordinary, and Somewhat Unusual SPINNING BOOK

No Batteries Required

Jimmy Huston

First Edition

Copyright © 2019 Jimmy Huston

ISBN 978-1-970022-49-0

All rights reserved, including the right to use or reproduce this book or portions thereof in any form whatsoever without written permission from the publisher except in the case of brief quotations embodied in critical articles or reviews.

Cosworth Publishing
21545 Yucatan Avenue
Woodland Hills, CA 91364
www.cosworthpublishing.com

For information regarding permission, please send an email to *office@cosworthpublishing.com*

Dedicated to reading dangerously.

Table of Contents

PART I..1

PART II..37

PART I

Chapter One

Nothing?

Huh...?

What about now?

Try making a sound with your mouth.

Maybe a sputtering engine
noise or a whirring spinning top...

Still nothing?

Keep trying. Maybe a different noise.

Aha! That works!

Keep going. You can do it!

What happened?

Did you stop making noise? Try again.

That's it! Keep it going!

You're getting the hang of it.

But you can't be straightening the book.

You've got to keep it going. Try again.

Nope. Are you making the noise?

Louder. Go for it!

Yes! That's working!

That's it! Keep it going!

When you turn the page,

feed the book through your fingers.

Yes, you're doing it. Don't stop!

You've done this before, haven't you?

Now speed it up. Read faster.

After all -- people are watching.

Is that as fast as you can read? Really?

And stop moving your lips.

When you get really good --

-- you can do this with your textbooks.

But you're not that good yet.

Okay -- STOP! But don't relax.

Now we're going in the other direction.

Oops. You know what this means.

You're not making your noises. Go!

That's it. Way to go!

Yikes. This way is harder.

Don't hurt yourself. Wheeeeeeeee!!!

Are you sure you can't read any faster?

Then skip the words and just turn the page.

At the end, there's going to be a test.

And remember. Whatever you do --

-- do NOT think about being dizzy.

It can be lots of fun to show this book to grownups.

Whew. Take a break. Catch your breath.

PART II

Chapter Two

The End

About the Author

He's too dizzy to finish...

Also by Jimmy Huston

The I Hate to Read Book

...and I Hate Math 2

Nate-Nate the Christmas Snake

The Dyslexic Handbook: Genius Edition

Cussing for Kids!: Etiquette for the Profane

The Attention Deficit Disorder Hyperactive Cookbook: Puzzle Edition

Autism for Beginners: Surfing the Spectrum

The OCD Funbook: Really?

The Bedtime Book of Bad Dreams: Dozing Dangerously

Baby's First Instruction Manual: How To Be the Center of the Universe

Rat BLEEP and Alien Poop: Not for Parents at All

The Big Beautiful Book of Burping, Belching, and Barfing

The Book Book: Inside the Inside Story

Why Can't Mommy Spend More Time with Me?

How to Write This Book: You're Going To Be the Author

That Damn Little Angel

The Snake Test: True? False? Maybe?

Is This Your First Funeral?: A Child's Primer

The First Apology Is the Worst

Don't Go to College, Go to Europe for Less

Dead Is the New Sick: An Insider's Guide to Senility, Paranoia, and Curmudgery

www.byjimmyhuston.com
www.cosworthpublishing.com

www.ingramcontent.com/pod-product-compliance
Lightning Source LLC
Chambersburg PA
CBHW081206020426
42333CB00020B/2631